English
Progress Papers 2

Patrick Berry and Susan Hamlyn

Schofield & Sims

Introduction

The **English Progress Papers** provide structured activities that increase in difficulty throughout the series, developing your knowledge and skills in English. Use the series to prepare for school entrance examinations, to improve your English knowledge and to practise a range of English skills.

How to use this book

There are six papers in this book. Each contains 85 questions, worth up to 100 marks. A single paper may take between 45 and 75 minutes to complete, and you might need two or more sessions to complete one paper.

For exam preparation, revision and all-round practice, work through the papers in order. Ask an adult helper to mark each paper, correct mistakes and explain where you went wrong. To practise a topic that you find challenging, work through selected activities in order of difficulty using the **Topics chart**, which is free to download from the Schofield & Sims website.

What does each paper contain?

Each paper is divided into three parts. Work carefully through each one and do not rush.

The **English skills** questions focus on key areas of grammar, punctuation and spelling and help you to avoid common mistakes. These questions will also expand your vocabulary, particularly if you incorporate the new words and phrases that you learn in to your own written work.

The multiple-choice **Comprehension** questions are not as easy as they look. Always read both the passage and the question carefully, particularly if all the answer options have some truth in them. One answer is always more accurate than the others, but careful thinking is needed to identify it.

The **Short writing task** is not designed as an extended piece of work and you will be able to complete some tasks in 20 to 30 minutes. Others may inspire you to write for longer – if you need more space, use separate sheets of paper. When working for a test or exam, restrict yourself to 30 minutes' writing, particularly in the last three months before the test. For ideas on how to tackle the different kinds of task, see **Short writing task tips**, which is free to download from the Schofield & Sims website.

Answers

The adult who is helping you will use the pull-out answer booklet to mark your work. If you get some questions wrong, check your answers against the correct answers given. Take time, with a dictionary and/or with an adult, to learn and remember why the answer given is correct. When checking a comprehension question, re-read carefully both the passage and the question and carefully think it through.

Use the **Progress chart** at the back of this book to record your marks and measure progress.

Downloads

Free downloads are available from the Schofield & Sims website (www.schofieldandsims.co.uk/free-downloads), including the resources mentioned above, extra practice material, guidance on alternative spellings and a glossary of English skills vocabulary.

Published by **Schofield & Sims Ltd**,
7 Mariner Court, Wakefield, West Yorkshire WF4 3FL, UK
Telephone 01484 607080
www.schofieldandsims.co.uk

First published in 1993
This edition copyright © Schofield & Sims Ltd, 2018
Second impression 2018

Authors: **Patrick Berry and Susan Hamlyn**

Patrick Berry and Susan Hamlyn have asserted their moral rights under the Copyright, Designs and Patents Act, 1988, to be identified as the authors of this work.

Grateful thanks to the Head and Year 6 pupils of Notting Hill and Ealing Junior School (GDST) for trialling **English Progress Papers** in their school.

British Library Cataloguing in Publication Data
A catalogue record for this book is available from the British Library.

All rights reserved. No part of this publication may be reproduced, stored in a retrieval system, or transmitted in any form or by any means, electronic, mechanical, photocopying, recording or otherwise, without either the prior permission of the publisher or a licence permitting restricted copying in the United Kingdom issued by the Copyright Licensing Agency Limited, Barnard's Inn, 86 Fetter Lane, London, EC4A 1EN.

Design by **Ledgard Jepson Ltd**

Printed in the UK by **Page Bros (Norwich) Ltd**

ISBN 978 07217 1474 5

Contents

Note for parents, tutors, teachers and other adult helpers

A pull-out answers section (pages A1 to A12) appears in the centre of this book, between pages 26 and 27 (Paper 9). This provides answers to all the **English skills** and **Comprehension** questions, as well as guidelines for marking the **Short writing tasks**. It also gives simple guidance on how best to use this book. Remove the pull-out section before the child begins working through the practice papers.

You may wish the child to have access to a dictionary – either while he or she is working through the papers or after you have marked them. Make a decision on this before the child begins work. You may also give the child some separate sheets of lined paper for continuing the **Short writing task** if needed.

START HERE

Q. 1–60 English skills

MARK

Q. 1–5
punctuation

Rewrite the sentence correctly, adding the necessary punctuation.

1 the visitors carrying a huge bouquet entered the room

_____

1 ☐ 1

2 im going to my friends stepmums on tuesday

_____

2 ☐ 1

3 monika attends st anselms rc primary school

_____

3 ☐ 1

4 where are you going asked marco

_____

4 ☐ 1

5 hasan said that our school was top of the league

_____

5 ☐ 1

Q. 6–10
word groups
(by meaning)

Write *one* word that may be used to describe all the others.

6 Dobermann, Rottweiler, Pekinese   _____

6 ☐ 1

7 Dutch, Hungarian, Gujarati   _____

7 ☐ 1

8 scalene, isosceles, equilateral   _____

8 ☐ 1

9 ravioli, spaghetti, penne   _____

9 ☐ 1

10 diplodocus, tyrannosaurus, triceratops _____

10 ☐ 1

Q. 11–15
past tense

Add to the sentence the past tense of the verb shown in capitals.

11 CHOOSE We _____ the brown puppy with floppy ears.

11 ☐ 1

12 BUY Dad _____ me the DVD I wanted.

12 ☐ 1

13 BLEED His cut leg _____ all over the carpet.

13 ☐ 1

14 BREAK I had to tell Mum that I'd _____ her watch.

14 ☐ 1

15 BRING Have you _____ your books with you?

15 ☐ 1

MARK ☐

English skills

MARK

Q. 16–20	Put the word in the sentence where it makes the best sense.	
word choice, homophones	wrapped, rapt, rapped, reek, wreak	

16 The teacher _____ on the desk.   16   1

17 The bull will _____ havoc in the china shop.   17   1

18 The baby was well _____ because it was cold.   18   1

19 The house will _____ of onions.   19   1

20 The children listened with _____ attention.   20   1

Q. 21–25	Write the popular phrase next to its meaning.
popular phrases	step into someone's shoes, all over the shop, money for old rope, to have money to burn, pigs might fly

21 to be very rich _____   21   1

22 it could never happen _____   22   1

23 easily earned _____   23   1

24 in a terrible mess _____   24   1

25 take over from somebody _____   25   1

Q. 26–30	Write the adjective formed from the noun.
adjectives	

26 atom   _____   26   1

27 biology   _____   27   1

28 hilarity   _____   28   1

29 tragedy   _____   29   1

30 stupidity   _____   30   1

MARK

English skills

MARK

Q. 31–35 spelling	Read the clue. Fill in the missing letters to make the word.		
	31 awake and alert	c _ _ _ c _ _ _ s	31 ☐ 1
	32 person living next door	n _ _ _ _ _ _ _ _	32 ☐ 1
	33 to vanish	d i s _ _ _ _ _ _	33 ☐ 1
	34 peace and calm	t _ _ _ _ _ _ _ _ _ _ y	34 ☐ 1
	35 the way we say words	p _ _ _ _ _ _ _ _ _ _ _ n	35 ☐ 1

Q. 36–40 word choice, prepositions	Four prepositions appear in brackets. Underline the *one* word that completes the sentence correctly.	
	36 My cat has a bug and is right (over, of, off, under) her food.	36 ☐ 1
	37 Your work is no different (against, from, between, for) mine.	37 ☐ 1
	38 She has been working here (for, after, before, since) 2014.	38 ☐ 1
	39 They have a real love (of, on, about, with) dogs.	39 ☐ 1
	40 That red belt contrasts well (against, to, with, on) your green shirt.	40 ☐ 1

Q. 41–45 nouns	Add to the sentence a noun that is made from the word shown in capitals.	
	41 DIZZY He had occasional _____ after the accident.	41 ☐ 1
	42 MODEST The dancer showed great _____ when interviewed.	42 ☐ 1
	43 INERT The day after the trip, the class was in a state of _____.	43 ☐ 1
	44 MEDIOCRE The _____ of the show was disappointing.	44 ☐ 1
	45 SANE The head solved the problem with humour and _____.	45 ☐ 1

MARK ☐

English skills

MARK

Q. 46–50 abbreviations	Write the words that the abbreviation (shortened form) stands for.		
	46 VIP _____	46	1
	47 BBC _____	47	1
	48 PTO _____	48	1
	49 NHS _____	49	1
	50 NB _____	50	1

Q. 51–55 plurals	Write the plural.		
	51 crisis _____	51	1
	52 oasis _____	52	1
	53 sheep _____	53	1
	54 basis _____	54	1
	55 loaf _____	55	1

Q. 56–60 similes	Put the word in the simile to which it belongs. mouse, nails, button, grass, mustard		
	56 as bright as a _____	56	1
	57 as hard as _____	57	1
	58 as quiet as a _____	58	1
	59 as hot as _____	59	1
	60 as green as _____	60	1

MARK

ENGLISH SKILLS SUB-TOTAL   60

Q. 61–75 Comprehension

MARK

Read this passage carefully.

Starlight and Streetlamps

Exploring some of the factors that affect your experience of being outdoors at night.

If you live in the countryside, you will know that you can go out on a clear night and the sky will be full of bright stars twinkling down at you. The stars and the moon can make quite a lot of light – enough
5 to see your way by, even if there are no streetlamps. On a cloudy night in the countryside, however, the stars seem to disappear and it can be so dark that you cannot see your own hand stretched out before you. If you are to leave your home at all you must
10 take a torch – and all country people ensure that the battery in their torch or phone is fully charged if they go out on a gloomy evening.

If you live in a city or town, you'll be used to well-lit roads, streetlamps studding the pavements and
15 light from windows and shops – even in the dark

of winter. Quite possibly, you will very seldom see the stars at all. Our streetlamps are mostly lit by electricity and they come on automatically when twilight arrives. It was not always so. Before
20 electricity, a lamplighter used to come down each road at evening with a long pole and a ladder. He would turn a lever that made gas come out of the top of the streetlamp and would light the lamp with his long pole. Some streets in London – notably
25 the area around the front of Buckingham Palace – are still lit by gas but, sadly, we no longer have lamplighters.

Now read these questions. You have a choice of four answers
to each question. Choose the *one* answer you think the best.
Draw a line in the box next to its letter, like this.

A ▭

61 What stops people who live in the countryside from seeing stars at night?

    A too many houses

    B clouds

    C trees

    D the moonlight

A ▭
B ▭
C ▭
D ▭   61   2

62 Which of the following words or phrases means the same as 'ensure' (line 10)?

    A find

    B worry

    C make certain

    D forget

A ▭
B ▭
C ▭
D ▭   62   2

63 Which word or phrase means the same as 'fully charged' (line 11)?

    A topped-up

    B very bright

    C of excellent quality

    D powerful

A ▭
B ▭
C ▭
D ▭   63   2

MARK ▭

Comprehension

MARK

64 Which of the following headings best fits the information in paragraph 1?

A The Dangers of Country Living A ☐

B The Night Sky in the Countryside B ☐

C The Power of the Stars C ☐

D Why You Should Always Have a Torch D ☐ **64** 2

65 Why is it sensible to take a torch with you if you go outdoors on a dark night?

A as a precaution A ☐

B as an instruction B ☐

C as an intention C ☐

D as a warning D ☐ **65** 2

66 Which of these sentences best describes the difference between living in the country and living in cities and towns?

A The countryside is always dark and towns are always light at night. A ☐

B There are no stars in towns and no streetlights in the countryside. B ☐

C Towns have electricity and the countryside does not. C ☐

D Nights are never dark in towns, whereas light at night in the countryside D ☐ **66** 2
depends on the weather.

67 Which of the following words or phrases means the same as 'come on automatically' (line 18)?

A come on suddenly A ☐

B come on immediately B ☐

C come on at a particular time C ☐

D are set to switch on by themselves D ☐ **67** 2

68 Which word below best describes the writer's feelings about the fact that there are no longer any lamplighters in towns?

A obstinate A ☐

B regretful B ☐

C relieved C ☐

D irritated D ☐ **68** 2

MARK

Comprehension

MARK

69 Which of the following phrases do you think best sums up the reason that stars are hard to see in cities?

A light pollution

B window displays

C climate change

D city life

A ☐
B ☐
C ☐
D ☐

69 ☐ 2

70 Which *one* of the following statements is definitely true?

A You can never see stars at night in cities.

B You can always see stars at night in the countryside.

C Our streetlights are all electric.

D There are no lamplighters now.

A ☐
B ☐
C ☐
D ☐

70 ☐ 2

71 Some people might feel nostalgic when reading this passage. Which of the following best defines the word 'nostalgia'?

A a feeling of illness or sickness

B a feeling of regret for the lost things of the past

C taking pleasure in nights and darkness

D an affection for the countryside

A ☐
B ☐
C ☐
D ☐

71 ☐ 2

Find the spelling mistake. Underline it and write the box letter at the end of the line.

72 In cities, there is   much arteficial   illumination, which   may be unnecessary.

　　　　　　A　　　　　　　　B　　　　　　　　C　　　　　　　　　D　　　　　　☐

72 ☐ 2

73 It can be dangerous   to negotiate   circuitous roads   in the nightime.

　　　　　　A　　　　　　　　B　　　　　　　C　　　　　　　　D　　　　　☐

73 ☐ 2

74 Everyone needs to   think carefully about   the responsable   use of electricity.

　　　　　　A　　　　　　　　B　　　　　　　C　　　　　　　　D　　　　　☐

74 ☐ 2

75 Lamplighting   is now an   obsolete   proffesion.

　　　　　　A　　　　　　　B　　　　　　　C　　　　　　　D　　　　　☐

75 ☐ 2

MARK ☐

COMPREHENSION SUB-TOTAL ☐ 30

Q. 76–85 Short writing task

MARK

Write for 20–30 minutes on *one* of the following. Continue on a separate sheet if you need to.

a) A Night Walk

b) Imagine you are a retired lamplighter. Write down some of your memories of doing your job.

c) Many people think that shops and other businesses should be made to switch off their lights at night to save electricity. Write a letter to your local newspaper arguing *either* for *or* against this idea.

END OF TEST

SHORT WRITING TASK SUB-TOTAL	10
English skills sub-total (from page 7)	60
Comprehension sub-total (from page 10)	30
Short writing task sub-total (from this page)	10
PAPER 7 TOTAL MARK	100

START HERE

Q. 1–60 English skills

MARK

Q. 1–5 punctuation	Rewrite the sentence correctly, adding the necessary punctuation.	
	1 this mosaic bought during our holiday is valuable	
	_____	1 ☐ 1
	2 every day at about this time my neighbour calls	
	_____	2 ☐ 1
	3 having seen the cat coming the girl poured some milk	
	_____	3 ☐ 1
	4 this film more than any other inspires me to become an actor _____	
	_____	4 ☐ 1
	5 spotting that the pizza had gone she called up to her son _____	
	_____	5 ☐ 1

Q. 6–10 verbs	Add to the sentence a verb that is made from the word shown in capitals.	
	6 MODERN It will be expensive to _____ the cottage.	6 ☐ 1
	7 JEOPARDY Drinking and driving _____ people's lives.	7 ☐ 1
	8 PROOF Can you _____ that I committed the crime?	8 ☐ 1
	9 BREATH The thick smoke made it difficult to _____.	9 ☐ 1
	10 PUBLICITY If you want a sell-out, you should _____ the show.	10 ☐ 1

Q. 11–15 spelling	Read the clue. Fill in the missing letters to make the word.	
	11 keeping on trying	p _ _ _ _ _ _ _ _ t	11 ☐ 1
	12 unimportant	i r _ _ _ _ _ _ _ _ t	12 ☐ 1
	13 something that belongs to someone	p _ _ _ _ _ _ _ _ n	13 ☐ 1
	14 a regular beat in music	r _ _ _ _ _ m	14 ☐ 1
	15 a play with a sad ending	t _ _ _ _ _ _ y	15 ☐ 1

MARK ☐

English skills

MARK

Q. 16–20	Write *one* word that may be used to describe all the others.		
word groups (by meaning)	16 alligator, crocodile, lizard, snake	_____	16 1
	17 gibbon, chimpanzee, gorilla, orang-utan	_____	17 1
	18 Cheddar, Brie, Danish Blue, Edam	_____	18 1
	19 greengage, satsuma, avocado, pawpaw	_____	19 1
	20 Poirot, Marple, Holmes, Morse	_____	20 1

Q. 21–25	The prefix *pre* means *before* as in *prefix*. Fill in the missing letters to make a word.		
prefixes, spelling	21 A time before dates were recorded is pre _ _ _ _ _ _ _ _.		21 1
	22 If people go before you, they pre _ _ _ _ you.		22 1
	23 Something that is decided beforehand is pre _ _ _ _ _ _ _ _ _ _.		23 1
	24 If you like something more than any others, you pre _ _ _ it.		24 1
	25 A short introduction at the start of a book is a pre _ _ _ _.		25 1

Q. 26–30	Write the *one* word that has *both* meanings.		
homonyms	26 to ignite / pale-coloured	_____	26 1
	27 to succeed in a test / to hand someone something	_____	27 1
	28 to start something off / motor boat	_____	28 1
	29 pipe for gas waste from an engine / to tire out	_____	29 1
	30 to hop from one foot to the other / huge container for rubbish	_____	30 1

MARK

English skills

MARK

Q. 31–35	Write the missing parts of speech of the word shown in capitals.					
parts of speech, nouns, adjectives, adverbs, verbs		NOUN	ADJECTIVE	ADVERB	VERB	
	Example:	SOFTNESS	*soft*	*softly*	*soften*	
	31	_____	_____	_____	LENGTHEN	31 ☐ 1
	32	_____	_____	HATEFULLY	_____	32 ☐ 1
	33	_____	CLEAN	_____	_____	33 ☐ 1
	34	_____	_____	SIMPLY	_____	34 ☐ 1
	35	HEAT	_____	_____	_____	35 ☐ 1

Q. 36–40	Two words appear in brackets. Underline the *one* word that completes the sentence correctly.	
word choice, homophones	36 My brother has just got his driving (licence, license).	36 ☐ 1
	37 What would you (advise, advice) me to do?	37 ☐ 1
	38 I'd do anything to avoid karate (practise, practice).	38 ☐ 1
	39 He has (devised, deviced) an interesting gadget.	39 ☐ 1
	40 I (prophecy, prophesy) rain on Thursday!	40 ☐ 1

Q. 41–45	Underline the *one* word that is the odd one out.	
odd one out (by meaning)	41 offspring, ancestors, progeny, heirs, descendants	41 ☐ 1
	42 tart, saccharine, acid, sharp, vinegary	42 ☐ 1
	43 bass, soloist, contralto, alto, tenor	43 ☐ 1
	44 veil, shawl, turban, beret, cap	44 ☐ 1
	45 torrent, drought, flood, deluge, downpour	45 ☐ 1

MARK ☐

English skills   MARK

Q. 46–50	Add the *one* missing word.		
word meanings	46 Someone who dies for a just or holy cause is a _____.	46	1
	47 Officials who represent their country abroad are _____.	47	1
	48 An artist who makes statues is a _____.	48	1
	49 The weaving of thread into fabric is done on a _____.	49	1
	50 The room in which a scientist works is a _____.	50	1

Q. 51–55	Unscramble the anagram to fit the meaning given.		
anagrams	51 RIVER ROSE (where water is stored) _____	51	1
	52 SIR LOOPY CHARM (where young children learn) _____ _____	52	1
	53 MESS THE VICAR (day before a winter festival) _____ _____	53	1
	54 CHEER PILOT (aircraft with rotating blades) _____	54	1
	55 TO BE DUD (wasn't sure) _____	55	1

Q. 56–60	Write down the antonym (opposite) of the word, using a prefix.		
prefixes, antonyms	56 audible _____	56	1
	57 inflate _____	57	1
	58 do _____	58	1
	59 efficient _____	59	1
	60 literate _____	60	1

MARK

ENGLISH SKILLS SUB-TOTAL   60

Q. 61–75 Comprehension

MARK

Read this passage carefully.

All Friends Together?

Joe and his friends are out for the day. But is all as it seems?

I was relieved. Sam had invited Mo along with us to the woods and I took that to mean that he wasn't angry with him any more. Mo seemed happier too, though I could tell he was still wary of Sam and just wanted to please him. We were going to build a camp, using the long branches that Sam and I had cut down the day before. It wasn't raining and Sam had the loops of rope we'd need to fortify the camp
5 and anchor it to the tree. He was carrying the knife too, although I didn't think we'd need it any more. It was tucked into its sheath and stuck out of his back pocket. Mo kept blowing his little whistle and I wished he wouldn't. It made him seem immature and I was sure Sam didn't like it. But Sam wasn't saying much.

Sam pushed ahead of Mo and me. He was breaking fiercely through the bushes and thrusting aside the
10 brambles and creepers that blocked the path. He didn't speak except to tell us, "This way," or "Pick up that branch," if a particularly springy one lay by the way. It wasn't quite the way I'd expected it to be – collaborative and fun. This felt more like a mission, an outing with a purpose, and I wasn't sure what that purpose was.

When we got to the camp, Mo was excited.
15 "What can I do?" he asked. "Let me be useful."
But Sam ignored him and just kicked the heap of branches to dislodge the leaves that had gathered overnight.
"We're going to need more long thin branches," he told me, "to weave in and out, to strengthen the foundations. You go and look."
20 "I'll go!" offered Mo, eagerly.
"No," responded Sam quickly. "Joe knows what we need."
"I'd better have the knife, then," I said.
"You won't need it," replied Sam. "Not for those thin branches."
I stood there. Something wasn't right. Sam's eyes glinted.
25 "Well, go on then," he muttered.

Now read these questions. You have a choice of four answers
to each question. Choose the *one* answer you think the best.
Draw a line in the box next to its letter, like this.

A ▭

61 What do you think has happened before the passage begins?

 A Mo and Joe have had a fight.
 B Sam and Joe have fallen out with each other.
 C Sam has upset Mo.
 D Mo has upset Sam.

61 ☐ 2

62 Mo is 'wary' of Sam (line 2). Which word or phrase below is closest in meaning to 'wary' as it is used here?

 A tired
 B on his guard with
 C terrified
 D not friendly to

62 ☐ 2

MARK ☐

Comprehension

MARK

63 'It wasn't raining and Sam had the rope we'd need to fortify the camp and anchor it to the tree' (lines 4–5). How many verbs or groups of verbs can you find in this sentence?

   A three   A ☐

   B two   B ☐

   C five   C ☐

   D four   D ☐   **63**   2

64 Which phrase best sums up Joe's feeling towards Mo in paragraph 1?

   A irritated and annoyed   A ☐

   B protective and anxious   B ☐

   C amused and friendly   C ☐

   D confident and considerate   D ☐   **64**   2

65 Which phrase below best describes Sam in paragraph 1?

   A aloof and inscrutable   A ☐

   B angry and mutinous   B ☐

   C adventurous and commanding   C ☐

   D pioneering and concentrating   D ☐   **65**   2

66 Joe says that 'It wasn't quite the way I'd expected it to be' (line 11). Which *one* of the following had he *not* expected of the outing?

   A to be led by one person   A ☐

   B to involve shared activity   B ☐

   C to include Mo   C ☐

   D to be pleasurable   D ☐   **66**   2

67 Which word best describes Sam's manner in paragraph 2?

   A auspicious   A ☐

   B authorial   B ☐

   C authoritarian   C ☐

   D armorial   D ☐   **67**   2

68 Which word best describes Joe's feelings by the end of paragraph 2?

   A superstitious   A ☐

   B incompetent   B ☐

   C impatient   C ☐

   D suspicious   D ☐   **68**   2

MARK

Comprehension

MARK

69 Which of the words below would best complete the sentence?

Sam doesn't want Joe to take the knife – and Joe finds this _____.

A annoying   A ☐
B unfriendly   B ☐
C disturbing   C ☐
D sensible   D ☐

69 | 2

70 Which word best describes how Joe thinks of Mo?

A silly   A ☐
B vulnerable   B ☐
C threatening   C ☐
D irritating   D ☐

70 | 2

71 Which of the words below would best complete the sentence?

At the end of the passage we are left in a state of _____.

A expense   A ☐
B suspense   B ☐
C intense   C ☐
D surprise   D ☐

71 | 2

Find the word that is used wrongly. Underline it and write the box letter at the end of the line.

72   Camp building, like   other team exercises,   depends on   neutral support.

         A   B   C   D   ☐

72 | 2

73 Sometimes in groups   of friends, one   powerful individual   presumes control.

         A   B   C   D   ☐

73 | 2

74 Joe discovers that   Sam's attentions are   different from those   he'd anticipated.

         A   B   C   D   ☐

74 | 2

75 Knives can be   indispensable but   are pretentiously lethal   in the wrong hands.

         A   B   C   D   ☐

75 | 2

MARK ☐

COMPREHENSION SUB-TOTAL ☐ 30

Q. 76–85 Short writing task

MARK

Write for 20–30 minutes on *one* of the following. Continue on a separate sheet if you need to.

a) It is later that evening and Joe is back home. Write his diary entry for that day.

b) Someone you know at school is being bullied. Write the conversation you have with your best friend in which you discuss how best to resolve the problem.

c) Describe in detail a walk in the woods. Think about the ways in which each of your senses responds to your surroundings.

_____

_____

_____

_____

_____

_____

_____

_____

_____

_____

_____

_____

_____

_____

_____

_____

_____

_____

_____

_____

_____

_____

_____

END OF TEST

SHORT WRITING TASK SUB-TOTAL	10
English skills sub-total (from page 15)	60
Comprehension sub-total (from page 18)	30
Short writing task sub-total (from this page)	10
PAPER 8 TOTAL MARK	100

Paper 9

Q. 1–60 English skills

MARK

Q. 1–5 punctuation	Rewrite the sentence correctly, adding the necessary punctuation. did you ever see sighed mrs mehta such an appalling page of handwriting in your entire life

1–5   5

Q. 6–10 word groups (by meaning)	Write *one* word that may be used to describe all the others.

6   oak, beech, birch, sycamore   6   1

7   Etna, Vesuvius, Krakatoa, Stromboli   7   1

8   apostrophe, colon, comma, hyphen   8   1

9   aren't, sci-fi, gym, CID   9   1

10   Malta, Ibiza, Wight, Crete   10   1

Q. 11–15 proverbs and sayings	Complete the proverb or saying.

11   Nothing ventured, _____ .   11   1

12   A leopard cannot _____ .   12   1

13   Strike while _____ .   13   1

14   When in Rome, _____ .   14   1

15   Take care of the pence _____

_____ .   15   1

MARK [ ]

English skills   MARK

Q. 16–20 prefixes, spelling	The prefix *sub* means *under*. Fill in the missing letters to make the word. 16 A thought that you are not aware of is in your sub _ _ _ _ _ _ _ _ _. 17 Under the sea is sub _ _ _ _ _ _. 18 Under the earth is sub _ _ _ _ _ _ _ _. 19 A tunnel for pedestrians is a sub _ _ _. 20 To put under the surface of water is to sub _ _ _ _ _.	16 1 17 1 18 1 19 1 20 1

Q. 21–25 popular phrases	Write the popular phrase next to its meaning. to sweep the board, to curry favour, to go the way of all flesh, like water off a duck's back, touch-and-go 21 having no effect _____ 22 to win everything _____ 23 to try to win attention _____ 24 to die _____ 25 risky _____	21 1 22 1 23 1 24 1 25 1

Q. 26–30 spelling	Read the clue. Fill in the missing letters to make the word. 26 necessary, essential i n d _ _ _ _ _ _ _ _ _ e 27 to give someone a place to stay a c c _ _ _ _ _ _ _ _ e 28 a place where you can eat r _ _ _ _ _ _ _ _ _ 29 within reach a c _ _ _ _ _ _ _ _ 30 to overstate or make big e x a _ _ _ _ _ _ _ _	26 1 27 1 28 1 29 1 30 1

MARK

English skills

MARK

Q. 31–35 adjectives	Underline the adjective(s).	
	31 Three hungry children sat at the bare table.	31 ☐ 1
	32 My young cousin is best friends with her sister.	32 ☐ 1
	33 There are new products on the site each day.	33 ☐ 1
	34 Which cushion did that destructive dog chew?	34 ☐ 1
	35 Fresh flowers will cheer up my convalescent mother.	35 ☐ 1

Q. 36–40 antonyms	Write down the antonym of the word.	
	36 eastwards _____	36 ☐ 1
	37 vaguely _____	37 ☐ 1
	38 finite _____	38 ☐ 1
	39 heavily _____	39 ☐ 1
	40 summit _____	40 ☐ 1

Q. 41–45 word choice	Three words appear in brackets. Underline the *one* word that completes the sentence correctly.	
	41 The meal was good so we thanked the (restauranteur, restaurateur, restorator).	41 ☐ 1
	42 The lazy footballer was (disinterested, misinterested, uninterested) in the result.	42 ☐ 1
	43 The hens have laid (less, fewer, lesser) eggs than yesterday.	43 ☐ 1
	44 Mum had to (mediate, meditate, medicate) between friends who were arguing.	44 ☐ 1
	45 Never (underestimate, overestimate, estimate) the care needed to raise children.	45 ☐ 1

MARK ☐

English skills

MARK

Q. 46–50 unscramble sentences	Unscramble the sentence so that it makes sense. Write the sentence on the line. Include capital letters and punctuation as needed.	

46 to parents comes are it sensible homework when my

_____

46   1

47 lessons i strange during hungry noises and get tummy my makes

_____

_____

47   1

48 tusks their people wicked elephants for kill

_____

48   1

49 they a wish were great i longer than are deal holidays

_____

49   1

50 my stretch stories i that like imagination

_____

50   1

Q. 51–55 homophones	Read the clues, then write the homophones.	

51 hurled _____ / royal seat _____

51   1

52 conceited _____ / weathercock _____

52   1

53 parent _____ / more distant _____

53   1

54 so you can hear it _____ / permitted _____

54   1

55 writing materials _____ / motionless _____

55   1

Q. 56–60 word groups (by meaning)	Underline the *one* word that may be used to describe all the others.	

56 asp, serpent, cobra, adder, python

56   1

57 wombat, kangaroo, koala, marsupial, wallaby

57   1

58 ram, bull, boar, king, male

58   1

59 nest, warren, habitation, sett, rookery

59   1

60 jelly, mousse, tart, dessert, pie

60   1

MARK

ENGLISH SKILLS SUB-TOTAL   60

Q. 61–75 Comprehension

MARK

Read this passage carefully.

MEET ONE OF BRITAIN'S MOST EXOTIC BIRDS
– a relatively new resident of London and Southern England.

Have you ever seen a rose-ringed parakeet? This bird's feathers are an exotic bright green – the colour of a Granny Smith apple – and it has a scarlet beak and orange-rimmed eyes. The 'rose-ring' refers to an attractive pinky-red band
5 that encircles its neck – a little like a tie, but without the part that hangs down. It has a very long pointed tail and emits a rasping shriek, which can make you jump if you're not used to it. It tends to fly in flocks, rather like a squadron of fighter jets. When a formation of eight or 10 zoom over you, all
10 squawking at once, it can feel a bit like being under attack. Its natural habitat is equatorial. It lives in both India and Africa but even if you have not seen it there, or in a zoo, you might have seen it in large numbers here in chilly England.

Sometime in the late 1980s someone or something in
15 England released a few parakeets into the open air. It might have been the Great Storm of October 1987 that did it – the south-east of England was devastated by a huge storm that uprooted trees in their thousands, upturned cars and battered houses. It is thought that someone's private aviary may have
20 been damaged in this extreme weather, and its inhabitants escaped to a (probably rather surprising) freedom in definitely *un*tropical England. You might have expected these poor immigrants to starve, given the fact that they had to survive on unfamiliar berries and nuts. However, they
25 have had a wonderful time, meeting, breeding, flourishing and alarming not just the local people but also the local birds whose habitat they have invaded.

It is now estimated that there are as many as 30,000 of these parakeets in and around London. There are smaller
30 populations elsewhere in the country. You can see them in gardens, on your bird table and in parks. Some people want them to be culled as they fear they will endanger our native birds. Others just enjoy this spectacle from warmer and more colourful climes as this species makes its home
35 among us.

Now read these questions. You have a choice of four answers to each question. Choose the *one* answer you think the best. Draw a line in the box next to its letter, like this.

A ▭

61 Which word best describes the parakeet's colour?

   A light
   B beautiful
   C fashionable
   D vivid

A ▢
B ▢
C ▢
D ▢   **61** ▢ 2

62 What do the words 'exotic' (title and line 2) and 'attractive' (line 4) suggest about the writer's view of parakeets?

   A that they are appealing to the eye
   B that they are strange and rare
   C that they are unusual and glossy
   D that they are strangely exciting

A ▢
B ▢
C ▢
D ▢   **62** ▢ 2

63 A 'Granny Smith' (lines 2–3) is a type of apple. Which of the following is *not* a type of apple?

   A Red Delicious
   B Bramley
   C Golden Sun
   D Cox

A ▢
B ▢
C ▢
D ▢   **63** ▢ 2

MARK ▢

Comprehension

MARK

64 Line 8 refers to a 'squadron' and line 9 refers to a 'formation'. Which of the following are these two words usually used to describe?

A birds of prey

B racing cars

C parachutists

D an aerial display performed by aircraft

A ☐
B ☐
C ☐
D ☐

64   2

65 Which word best describes the experience of having a flock of parakeets flying overhead (see paragraph 1)?

A intimidating

B picturesque

C colourful

D noisy

A ☐
B ☐
C ☐
D ☐

65   2

66 Which of these words from paragraph 1 tells us most clearly that the parakeets come from hot countries?

A rose-ringed

B exotic

C equatorial

D habitat

A ☐
B ☐
C ☐
D ☐

66   2

67 How many verbs or groups of verbs can you find in the second sentence of paragraph 2?

A six

B four

C ten

D seven

A ☐
B ☐
C ☐
D ☐

67   2

68 Line 16 refers to a Great Storm. Which of the following is *not* a type of storm?

A tempest

B tycoon

C tornado

D cyclone

A ☐
B ☐
C ☐
D ☐

68   2

69 Which *one* phrase most accurately describes the most likely reason for the parakeets' arrival in Southern England?

A an accident in 1987

B their arrival from the tropics

C they came from abroad during the Great Storm

D someone or something let them into the wild

A ☐
B ☐
C ☐
D ☐

69   2

MARK

Comprehension

MARK

70 Why are the parakeets described as 'immigrants' (line 23)?

A because of their colour
B because they have arrived from abroad
C because they are poor
D because they are free

A
B
C
D   70 2

71 We are told that the parakeets 'have had a wonderful time' (line 25). From your reading of the passage, select *two* reasons for this.
1. their numbers have greatly increased   3. they like bird tables
2. they have adapted to our climate   4. they frighten other birds

A 1 and 4
B 2 and 3
C 1 and 2
D 3 and 4

A
B
C
D   71 2

72 Identify the types of words contained in the sentence 'There are smaller populations elsewhere in the country' (lines 29–30).

A two nouns, two verbs and an adjective
B one noun, one verb and two adjectives
C two nouns, one verb and an adverb
D two nouns, one verb, one adjective and one adverb

A
B
C
D   72 2

73 While some people 'fear' the parakeets, others 'enjoy' them (lines 32–33). Which word best describes these two attitudes?

A conventional
B contrasting
C consistent
D controversial

A
B
C
D   73 2

74 Which word is the odd one out?

A emigrant
B migrate
C immigrant
D migrant

A
B
C
D   74 2

75 Which word does *not* refer to the noise parakeets can make?

A rasping
B squawking
C zoom
D flourishing

A
B
C
D   75 2

MARK

COMPREHENSION SUB-TOTAL   30

English
Progress Papers 2
Answers

Schofield&Sims

English Progress Papers 2

Notes for parents, tutors, teachers and other helpers

This pull-out book contains correct answers to all the questions in **English Progress Papers 2**, and is designed to assist you, the adult helper, as you mark the child's work. Once the child has become accustomed to the method of working, you may wish to give him or her direct access to this pull-out section.

When marking, write the number of marks achieved in the tinted column on the far right of the question page. The number to the right of the white mark box indicates the maximum mark available for that question. Sub-total boxes at the foot of each page will help you to add marks quickly. You can then fill in the total marks at the end of the paper. Here you can record separately the child's score in each of the three parts of the paper. The total score is out of 100 and therefore yields a percentage result. The child's progress can be recorded using the **Progress chart** on page 52.

Each paper is divided into three sections, as follows.

	Number of questions	Total marks available	Approximate time available
English skills	60	60	10–20 minutes
Comprehension	15	30	15–25 minutes
Short writing task	The child chooses and completes one of three tasks, for which 10 marks may be gained.	10	20–30 minutes
Totals	**85 questions**	**100 marks**	**45–75 minutes**

English skills (60 questions, worth a total of 60 marks)

This first section comprises 12 groups of five brief questions. In **English Progress Papers 2**, you can expect children to take between 10 and 20 minutes to complete it. Each group of questions tests a particular area of literacy skill or knowledge. Most of the questions in this first section have right or wrong answers (for example, the past tense of *buy* is *bought*). However, some do not and a range of answers is possible. If the question asks, for example, for a sentence to be changed from indirect to direct speech then some variation from the suggested answer is acceptable. You must make your own judgement concerning these questions.

The questions in this section are worth one mark if answered correctly. The only exception is the somewhat longer punctuation question at the start of papers 9, 11 and 12, which is allocated a maximum of five marks. In all questions like these, where the right answer includes several different elements, give full marks only if the response is completely correct and covers all the constituent parts.

Some English words can be spelt correctly in more than one way. For a free download providing notes and guidance on alternative spellings, visit the Schofield & Sims website.

Comprehension (15 questions, worth a total of 30 marks)

The second section offers passages for comprehension followed by 15 multiple-choice questions, each with a choice of four possible answers – only one of which should be chosen. The Comprehension section in this book should take children between 15 and 25 minutes to answer. The questions vary in difficulty, but you should tell the child to assume that they are more difficult than they might at first appear. Encourage the child to read carefully both the passage and the question before answering. Sometimes, the distinction between several of the possible answers offered is subtle: care and re-reading of both the passage and the question may be needed before the choice is made.

A correctly answered Comprehension question is worth two marks. This reflects the importance of these questions, which test understanding of the passage as well as grammar and spelling.

Short writing task (worth a total of 10 marks)

The third section allows the child between 20 and 30 minutes to write a brief composition on one of three topics. Space is available for the piece of writing to be written on the page, directly below the list of topics. However, the child may need an extra sheet of paper on which to continue, so be sure to have some available.

Marking a child's composition is not an exact science, but generally speaking you should give credit for strengths and deduct marks for deficiencies. The guidelines below will help you to give the child's writing a mark out of 10. Please bear in mind that, at this level, it should not be impossible for a lively and accurately written piece to gain full marks.

Where an essay title is provided, this may be interpreted exactly as the child wishes. For example, the title 'The Great Storm' (Paper 9, option a), could prompt the child to write a fictional story or a newspaper report. In total, this series provides 54 essay topics, requiring a range of writing skills and styles as listed opposite, used for a variety of purposes and aimed at different readers. Help the child to understand that not all writing is the same: they would not write a thank-you letter to their grandparents in the same style as a speech to be read out in class or a story for a younger child.

Give credit for:	Deduct marks for:
• writing in a style appropriate to the task and audience (see table opposite)	• inappropriate style – for example, too formal or informal for purpose and/or audience (see table opposite)
• correct spelling and punctuation, legible handwriting	• poor spelling and/or illegibility
• appropriate use of paragraphing and the setting out of dialogue	• inadequate or misplaced punctuation, paragraphing, use of capital letters
• correct grammar (allow some leeway for, for example, colloquial conversation, especially if it is expressive of individual character)	• writing that loses its way, is irrelevant to the title, doesn't make sense or is repetitive
• consistency within the piece of writing in the use of verb tenses	• inconsistent use of verb tenses – moving from past to present or vice versa
• use of interesting, varied and lively vocabulary	• inconsistent narrative approach – for example, changing from third person to first person or changing tenses mid-narrative
• narrative, descriptive or explicatory flair – for example, in holding the reader's attention, story twists, imaginative use of language	• a sense that the writer is not in control and is either struggling to write enough or struggling to contain an idea that is too big for the time allowed
• an overall sense of control and confidence	

The table opposite highlights different aspects of style – arranged by task type and designed to help you as you mark different types of writing. Discourage the child from always choosing the 'story' option. The experience of tackling the varied writing tasks provided in this series will give the child the skills and confidence to write well – not just in English tests but in all other aspects of study and life where writing matters.

Task type	Book 2	
Story writing • A 30-minute time limit does not allow for a large cast or for several changes of place and day. The story will work best if the action happens all in one go, in one location and with only a few participants. • It is best for the child to avoid a long introduction, unless it is vital to the story. Award an extra mark if the child plunges straight into the story. This is particularly important, of course, if the child has been asked to continue the story where it left off or to write from a particular character's viewpoint. • Even bearing in mind these limitations, you may still find pace, dialogue and description that helps you to imagine the events, setting and atmosphere.	Paper 7a) Paper 8a) Paper 9a)	Paper 10b)
Concise description • Look for evidence that the child has taken account of the intended audience for the piece of writing and adjusted his or her style accordingly. • For example, if the piece of writing requested is for a website or magazine, look for a concise style that will keep the attention of readers: watch out for too much detail, particularly any facts that are irrelevant to the audience.	Paper 9a)	Paper 12a)
Detailed description • Where a full description is required, give marks for clearly imagined and carefully crafted prose. • Look for descriptions that give a strong sense of the person, place or thing.	Paper 7a) Paper 7b) Paper 8c) Paper 9b)	Paper 10a) Paper 11a) Paper 11b)
Instructions, persuasive writing and explanations • Clarity of thinking makes for clarity of expression. Before the child starts writing, he or she needs first to identify the purpose of the piece of writing. • *Instructions* need to be simple, correctly ordered and straightforward. • *Writing that aims to persuade or to influence* should avoid nagging or insulting the reader. Carefully worked-out arguments – clearly expressed and with separate points that are logically ordered – can be very effective. • *Explanation* must be clearly focused on exactly what it is that the reader needs to understand. Always look for evidence that the child understands what he or she is trying to explain. You cannot provide a clear explanation of something that you do not understand.	Paper 7c)	Paper 10c) Paper 11b) Paper 11c)
Discussion • As above, look for clarity of thinking and expression, as well as evidence that the child has some understanding of the issue under discussion. • Strong opinions are not needed: being able to see several sides to a question is a valuable skill. • Simple sentences may work best in writing of this kind.	Paper 9c)	Paper 12c)
Conversation and dialogue • Some questions invite the child to write a conversation, develop or create one or more characters, or speak in the voice of a particular character. Since we do not all speak in the same way, written conversation should convey a sense of the speaker, the context and the subject matter. • All conversation should be correctly set out and punctuated.	Paper 7b) Paper 8a) Paper 8b)	Paper 11a) Paper 12b)

Paper 7
English skills

1 | The visitors, carrying a huge bouquet, entered the room.
This sentence would also be correct were the commas removed, though this would slightly change the meaning.

2 | I'm going to my friend's stepmum's on Tuesday.
3 | Monika attends St Anselm's RC Primary School.
4 | "Where are you going?" asked Marco.
5 | Hasan said that our school was top of the league.

6 | dog
7 | language *or* nationality
8 | triangle
9 | pasta
10 | dinosaur

11 | chose
12 | bought
13 | bled
14 | broken
15 | brought

16 | rapped
17 | wreak
18 | wrapped
19 | reek
20 | rapt

21 | to have money to burn
22 | pigs might fly
23 | money for old rope
24 | all over the shop
25 | step into someone's shoes

26 | atomic
27 | biological
28 | hilarious
29 | tragic
30 | stupid

Paper 7 – *continued*

31 | conscious
32 | neighbour
33 | disappear
34 | tranquillity
35 | pronunciation

36 | off
37 | from
38 | since
39 | of
40 | with

41 | dizziness
42 | modesty
43 | inertia
44 | mediocrity
45 | sanity

46 | Very Important Person
47 | British Broadcasting Corporation
48 | Please Turn Over
49 | National Health Service
50 | Nota Bene (*meaning 'note well'*)

51 | crises
52 | oases
53 | sheep
54 | bases
55 | loaves

56 | button
57 | nails
58 | mouse
59 | mustard
60 | grass

Paper 7 – *continued*
Comprehension

61 | B
62 | C
63 | A
64 | B
65 | A
66 | D
67 | D
68 | B
69 | A
70 | D
71 | B
72 | B arteficial (*should be 'artificial'*)
73 | D nightime (*should be 'night-time'*)
74 | C responsable (*should be 'responsible'*)
75 | D proffesion (*should be 'profession'*)

Short writing task

Refer to general guidelines on page A4 and specific notes on page A5 as indicated.

a) | Detailed description, Story writing
b) | Conversation and dialogue, Detailed description
c) | Instructions, persuasive writing and explanations

Paper 8
English skills

1 | This mosaic, bought during our holiday, is valuable.
2 | Every day, at about this time, my neighbour calls. *This sentence would also be correct were the commas removed, though this would slightly change the meaning.*
3 | Having seen the cat coming, the girl poured some milk.
4 | This film, more than any other, inspires me to become an actor. *This sentence would also be correct were the commas removed, though this would slightly change the meaning.*
5 | Spotting that the pizza had gone, she called up to her son.

6 | modernise
7 | jeopardise
8 | prove
9 | breathe
10 | publicise

11 | persistent
12 | irrelevant
13 | possession
14 | rhythm
15 | tragedy

16 | reptile
17 | ape
18 | cheese
19 | fruit
20 | detective

21 | prehistoric
22 | precede
23 | predetermined
24 | prefer
25 | preface

Paper 8 – *continued*

26 | light
27 | pass
28 | launch
29 | exhaust
30 | skip

31 | length, long, lengthily, (lengthen)
32 | hate *or* hatred, hateful, (hatefully), hate
33 | cleanliness *or* cleaner (*in the sense of 'a person who cleans'*), (clean), cleanly, clean *or* cleanse
34 | simplicity *or* simplification *or* simpleton, simple, (simply), simplify
35 | (heat), hot *or* heated, hotly, heat

36 | licence
37 | advise
38 | practice
39 | devised
40 | prophesy

41 | ancestors
42 | saccharine
43 | soloist
44 | shawl
45 | drought

46 | martyr
47 | ambassadors *or* diplomats
48 | sculptor
49 | loom
50 | laboratory

51 | reservoir
52 | primary school
53 | Christmas Eve
54 | helicopter
55 | doubted

56 | inaudible
57 | deflate
58 | undo
59 | inefficient
60 | illiterate

Paper 8 – *continued*
Comprehension

61 | D
62 | B
63 | C
64 | B
65 | A
66 | A
67 | C
68 | D
69 | C
70 | B
71 | B
72 | D neutral (*should be 'mutual'*)
73 | D presumes (*should be 'assumes'*)
74 | B attentions (*should be 'intentions'*)
75 | C pretentiously (*should be 'potentially'*)

Short writing task

Refer to general guidelines on page A4 and specific notes on page A5 as indicated.

a) | Story writing, Conversation and dialogue
b) | Conversation and dialogue
c) | Detailed description

Paper 9
English skills

1–5	"Did you ever see," sighed Mrs Mehta, "such an appalling page of handwriting in your entire life?"
6	tree
7	volcano
8	punctuation (mark)
9	abbreviation
10	island
11	nothing gained
12	change its spots
13	the iron is hot
14	do as the Romans (do)
15	and the pounds will take care of themselves
16	subconscious
17	submarine
18	subterranean
19	subway
20	submerge
21	like water off a duck's back
22	to sweep the board
23	to curry favour
24	to go the way of all flesh
25	touch-and-go
26	indispensable
27	accommodate
28	restaurant
29	accessible
30	exaggerate
31	Three hungry children sat at the bare table.
32	My young cousin is best friends with her sister.
33	There are new products on the site each day.
34	Which cushion did that destructive dog chew?
35	Fresh flowers will cheer up my convalescent mother.

Paper 9 – *continued*

36	westwards
37	precisely *or* certainly *or* definitely *or* exactly
38	infinite
39	lightly
40	base *or* bottom *or* nadir *or* valley *or* trough
41	restaurateur
42	uninterested
43	fewer
44	mediate
45	underestimate
46	My parents are sensible when it comes to homework.
47	I get hungry during lessons and my tummy makes strange noises.
48	Wicked people kill elephants for their tusks.
49	I wish holidays were a great deal longer than they are.
50	I like stories that stretch my imagination.
51	thrown/throne
52	vain/vane
53	father/farther
54	aloud/allowed
55	stationery/stationary
56	serpent
57	marsupial
58	male
59	habitation
60	dessert

Paper 9 – *continued*
Comprehension

61	D
62	A
63	C
64	D
65	A
66	C
67	A
68	B
69	A
70	B
71	C
72	D
73	B
74	B
75	D

Short writing task

Refer to general guidelines on page A4 and specific notes on page A5 as indicated.

a)	Story writing, Concise description
b)	Detailed description
c)	Discussion

Paper 10
English skills

1 | You're not going to bed yet, are you?
2 | "These cans' labels have come off," Alison groaned.
3 | The children's parents attended the headteacher's talk.
4 | Mr Johns told me to collect the laptops, put them away and run back.
5 | "Eat breakfast," said Mum, "before you go out to play."

6 | Royal Society for the Prevention of Cruelty to Animals
7 | Criminal Investigation Department
8 | Saint *or* Street
9 | Frequently asked questions
10 | electronic mail

11 | arachnophobia
12 | agoraphobia
13 | hydrophobia
14 | claustrophobia
15 | xenophobia

16 | Hanoverian
17 | Victorian
18 | Elizabethan
19 | Manx
20 | Georgian

21 | southern
22 | smooth
23 | immortal
24 | permanent
25 | majority

26 | uninteresting
27 | serious
28 | transparent *or* translucent
29 | mischievous
30 | colossal

Paper 10 – *continued*

31 | truancy *or* truanting
32 | parallelogram
33 | pavement *or* paving
34 | heroism
35 | emotion

36 | croquet
37 | ravine
38 | diminutive
39 | reality
40 | Gemini

41 | device
42 | licence
43 | luxuriant
44 | vain
45 | deferred

46 | benefactor
47 | beneficial
48 | benevolent *or* beneficent
49 | beneficiary
50 | benefit

51 | flea/flee
52 | oar/ore
53 | whole/hole
54 | cue/queue
55 | links/lynx

56 | to have sticky fingers
57 | to stir your stumps
58 | to send somebody packing
59 | to pass the hat round
60 | to live from hand to mouth

Paper 10 – *continued*
Comprehension

61 | C
62 | C
63 | A
64 | A
65 | D
66 | A
67 | C
68 | B
69 | A
70 | D
71 | A
72 | B
73 | C
74 | D
75 | B

Short writing task

Refer to general guidelines on page A4 and specific notes on page A5 as indicated.

a) | Detailed description
b) | Story writing
c) | Instructions, persuasive writing and explanations

Paper 11
English skills

1–5 | "I'm not sure I'll be able to come to Monday's party, Kamran," sighed the boy. "I'm afraid I've got a dental appointment at Mr Melton's surgery in Oakwood."

6 | toughened
7 | donated *or* donate
8 | ripen
9 | mistook
10 | pacify

11 | blue
12 | fiddle
13 | flight
14 | bark
15 | nag

16 | sapling
17 | caddy
18 | spectators *or* crowd
19 | jockey
20 | decade

21 | Josh asked when the last bus was (due). *or* Josh asked what time the last bus was. *or* Josh asked (for) the time of the last bus.
22 | The stranger asked me the way to the Town Hall.
23 | Nandita asked (me) whether (*or* if) they were my gloves.
24 | The lady in the wheelchair asked me to reach the biscuits for her.
25 | Prince Charming asked Cinderella to marry him.

26 | Hertfordshire
27 | South Yorkshire
28 | Gloucestershire
29 | Cambridgeshire
30 | Leicestershire

Paper 11 – *continued*

31 | rooted to the spot
32 | a square peg in a round hole
33 | lead the life of Riley
34 | not to be sneezed at
35 | done to a turn

36 | privilege
37 | yacht
38 | marriage
39 | definitely
40 | February

41 | She came <u>early</u> and spoke <u>first</u>.
42 | "I'm late!" shouted Mum, running <u>fast</u> down the path.
43 | He walks <u>well</u> but is in some pain.
44 | He is a <u>very</u> old man and walks <u>slowly</u>.
45 | <u>There</u> is the spot where the horse fell <u>heavily</u>.

46 | is another man's poison
47 | is not gold
48 | and half a dozen of the other
49 | wait for no man
50 | but it pours

51 | A second series of plays <u>is</u> being planned.
52 | The escaped herd of cows <u>is</u> on the motorway.
53 | A bunch of flowers <u>is</u> just what Mia needs.
54 | The team <u>was</u> driving through town on an open-top bus.
55 | The crew <u>is</u> in a state of shock.

56 | committee
57 | dedicated
58 | beginning
59 | murmur
60 | independent

Paper 11 – *continued*
Comprehension

61 | D
62 | B
63 | B
64 | C
65 | A
66 | A
67 | D
68 | B
69 | C
70 | D
71 | B
72 | C bisiness (*should be 'business'*)
73 | B biuld (*should be 'build'*)
74 | C spesialist (*should be 'specialist'*)
75 | C truely (*should be 'truly'*)

Short writing task

Refer to general guidelines on page A4 and specific notes on page A5 as indicated.

a) | Detailed description, Conversation and dialogue
b) | Detailed description, Instructions, persuasive writing and explanations
c) | Instructions, persuasive writing and explanations

Paper 12
English skills

1–5	"The play," said Paola, "is 'The Importance of Being Earnest' by Oscar Wilde. Have you seen it? It's very funny."
6	red
7	blue
8	black
9	violet/lilac/purple
10	green
11	left
12	drama
13	tooth
14	scooter
15	porch
16	to give up the ghost
17	to push one's luck
18	to pull through
19	to drown one's sorrows
20	out of the woods
21	espionage
22	illegal *or* illicit
23	telepathy
24	conservation
25	lava *or* magma
26	Northumbrian
27	Cumbrian
28	Belgian
29	Spanish
30	Welsh
31	"Pass it to me!" *or* "Pass me the ball!" *or* "Pass the ball to me!" shouted Joanna.
32	"When's dinner ready, Dad?" asked Navid. *or* "When's dinner ready?" Navid asked Dad. *or* "When will dinner be ready, Dad?" asked Navid.
33	"I hope my career will be on stage rather than in films," *or* "I hope to work on stage, rather than in films," said the actor.

Paper 12 – *continued*

34	"Would you like to come with us on holiday?" *or* "We'd like you to come with us on holiday," said Ailsa's mum.
35	"I've left my boots in the car," admitted Karl.
36	dissatisfied *or* disappointed
37	awkward
38	journey
39	disappear
40	changeable
41	bigamously
42	hungrily
43	brutally
44	enigmatically
45	eerily
46	wintry *or* wintery
47	rightful
48	health
49	ignorance
50	wealth *or* riches
51	undertaker
52	surgeon
53	IT manager
54	steward
55	bursar
56	triangle
57	triathlon
58	tricolour *or* tricolore
59	tricycle
60	trident

Paper 12 – *continued*

Comprehension

61	D
62	B
63	A
64	C
65	D
66	B
67	C
68	B
69	D
70	B
71	D
72	B opportunaty (*should be 'opportunity'*)
73	B airborn (*should be 'airborne'*)
74	C suprise (*should be 'surprise'*)
75	C definate (*should be 'definite'*)

Short writing task

Refer to general guidelines on page A4 and specific notes on page A5 as indicated.

a)	Concise description
b)	Conversation and dialogue
c)	Discussion

This book of answers is a pull-out section from
English Progress Papers 2

Published by **Schofield & Sims Ltd**,
7 Mariner Court, Wakefield, West Yorkshire WF4 3FL, UK
Telephone 01484 607080
www.schofieldandsims.co.uk

First published in 1993
This edition copyright © Schofield & Sims Ltd, 2018
Second impression 2018

Authors: **Patrick Berry and Susan Hamlyn**
Patrick Berry and Susan Hamlyn have asserted their moral rights
under the Copyright, Designs and Patents Act, 1988, to be identified
as the authors of this work.

British Library Cataloguing in Publication Data
A catalogue record for this book is available from the British Library.

All rights reserved. No part of this publication may be reproduced, stored in
a retrieval system, or transmitted in any form or by any means, electronic,
mechanical, photocopying, recording or otherwise, without either the prior
permission of the publisher or a licence permitting restricted copying in
the United Kingdom issued by the Copyright Licensing Agency Limited,
Barnard's Inn, 86 Fetter Lane, London EC4A 1EN.

Design by **Ledgard Jepson Ltd**

Printed in the UK by **Page Bros (Norwich) Ltd**

ISBN 978 07217 1474 5

Q. 76–85 Short writing task

MARK

Write for 20–30 minutes on *one* of the following. Continue on a separate sheet if you need to.

a) The Great Storm

b) Describe an animal or bird that you know well, remembering to include details about how it moves, what it eats and the sounds that it makes.

c) The parakeets living in England are an 'invasive' species – that is, they do not originate from the UK. Because the species could wipe out other animals and birds, many people would like to reduce the numbers of these birds. What do you think about this? Do you think there should be any control over the populations of invasive species?

_____

END OF TEST

SHORT WRITING TASK SUB-TOTAL	10
English skills sub-total (from page 23)	60
Comprehension sub-total (from page 26)	30
Short writing task sub-total (from this page)	10
PAPER 9 TOTAL MARK	100

Paper 10

Q. 1–60 English skills

MARK

Q. 1–5 punctuation	Rewrite the sentence correctly, adding the necessary punctuation.	

1 youre not going to bed yet are you

_____ | **1** ☐ 1

2 these cans labels have come off alison groaned

_____ | **2** ☐ 1

3 the childrens parents attended the headteachers talk

_____ | **3** ☐ 1

4 mr johns told me to collect the laptops put them away and run back

_____

_____ | **4** ☐ 1

5 eat breakfast said mum before you go out to play

_____ | **5** ☐ 1

Q. 6–10 abbreviations	Write the words that the abbreviation stands for.

6 RSPCA _____ | **6** ☐ 1

7 CID _____ | **7** ☐ 1

8 St _____ or _____ | **8** ☐ 1

9 FAQ _____ | **9** ☐ 1

10 e-mail _____ | **10** ☐ 1

Q. 11–15 word meanings	A phobia is a very strong fear. Write each of the given phobias next to its meaning.

claustrophobia, xenophobia, agoraphobia, hydrophobia, arachnophobia

11 fear of spiders _____ | **11** ☐ 1

12 fear of open spaces _____ | **12** ☐ 1

13 fear of water _____ | **13** ☐ 1

14 fear of enclosed spaces _____ | **14** ☐ 1

15 fear of strangers or foreigners _____ | **15** ☐ 1

MARK ☐

    Schofield & Sims • English Progress Papers 2

English skills

MARK

Q. 16–20	Add to the sentence an adjective that is made from the noun shown in capitals.		
adjectives	16 HANOVER Queen Victoria was Britain's last _____ monarch.	16	1
	17 VICTORIA In _____ times, British industry was very powerful.	17	1
	18 ELIZABETH In _____ times, explorers sailed all over the world.	18	1
	19 MAN (The Isle of) The _____ cat has no tail.	19	1
	20 GEORGE Our museum has beautiful pieces of _____ silver.	20	1

Q. 21–25	Write down the antonym of the word.		
antonyms	21 northern _____	21	1
	22 rough _____	22	1
	23 mortal _____	23	1
	24 temporary _____	24	1
	25 minority _____	25	1

Q. 26–30	Read the clue. Fill in the missing letters to make the word.		
spelling	26 boring u n i n t _ _ _ _ _ _ _ _	26	1
	27 solemn or unsmiling s _ _ _ _ _ _	27	1
	28 see-through t _ _ _ s _ _ _ _ _ _	28	1
	29 naughty m _ _ c h _ _ _ _ _ _	29	1
	30 enormous c o _ _ _ _ _ l	30	1

MARK

English skills   MARK

Q. 31–35 nouns	Add to the sentence a noun that is made from the word shown in capitals.	
	31 TRUANT Matt's _____ got his parents into trouble.	31 ☐ 1
	32 PARALLEL I used a ruler to draw this _____.	32 ☐ 1
	33 PAVE Please walk on the _____ and not on the road.	33 ☐ 1
	34 HEROIC The police officer was awarded a medal for her _____.	34 ☐ 1
	35 EMOTIONAL There was great _____ when the men were rescued.	35 ☐ 1

Q. 36–40 odd one out (by meaning)	Underline the *one* word that is the odd one out.	
	36 minim, quaver, crotchet, croquet, breve	36 ☐ 1
	37 brook, ravine, stream, tributary, burn	37 ☐ 1
	38 titanic, prodigious, mammoth, elephantine, diminutive	38 ☐ 1
	39 hallucination, mirage, reality, dream, illusion	39 ☐ 1
	40 Venus, Neptune, Gemini, Mars, Jupiter	40 ☐ 1

Q. 41–45 word choice	Two words appear in brackets. Underline the *one* word that completes the sentence correctly.	
	41 He invented a new (device, devise) for opening cans.	41 ☐ 1
	42 He has a (license, licence) to sell tobacco.	42 ☐ 1
	43 The explorer hacked through the (luxuriant, luxurious) undergrowth.	43 ☐ 1
	44 They waited in (vain, vein, vane) for the bus to come.	44 ☐ 1
	45 The barrister (differed, deferred) to the wishes of the judge.	45 ☐ 1

MARK ☐

English skills

MARK

Q. 46–50	The prefix *bene* means *good* or *well*. Fill in the missing letters to make the word.		
prefixes, spelling	46 A person who helps by providing money is a bene _ _ _ _ _ _.	46	1
	47 Something which is good for you is bene _ _ _ _ _ _.	47	1
	48 Someone kind or generous is bene _ _ _ _ _ _.	48	1
	49 If you receive money from a will you are a bene _ _ _ _ _ _ _.	49	1
	50 Something that does you good or is of value to you is a bene _ _ _.	50	1

Q. 51–55	Read the clues, then write the homophones.		
homophones	51 small hopping insect _____ / to run away or escape _____	51	1
	52 used to row a boat _____ / valuable rock _____	52	1
	53 all of something _____ / a gap or missing part _____	53	1
	54 used when playing snooker _____ / line of people waiting _____	54	1
	55 connections _____ / animal of the cat family _____	55	1

Q. 56–60	Write the popular phrase next to its meaning.		
popular phrases	to live from hand to mouth, to send somebody packing, to pass the hat round, to have sticky fingers, to stir your stumps		
	56 to be likely to steal _____	56	1
	57 to hurry up or get going _____	57	1
	58 to tell somebody forcefully to leave _____	58	1
	59 to collect money for a cause _____	59	1
	60 to survive as best you can _____	60	1

MARK

ENGLISH SKILLS SUB-TOTAL

60

Q. 61–75 Comprehension

MARK

Read this passage carefully.

My Shadow

I have a little shadow that goes in and out with me,
And what can be the use of him is more than I can see.
He is very, very like me from the heels up to the head;
And I see him jump before me, when I jump into my bed.

5 The funniest thing about him is the way he likes to grow –
Not at all like proper children, which is always very slow;
For he sometimes shoots up taller like an india-rubber ball,
And he sometimes gets so little that there's none of him at all.

He hasn't got a notion of how children ought to play,
10 And can only make a fool of me in every sort of way.
He stays so close beside me, he's a coward you can see;
I'd think shame to stick to Mummy as that shadow sticks to me!

One morning, very early, before the sun was up,
I rose and found the shining dew on every buttercup;
15 But my lazy little shadow, like an arrant sleepy-head,
Had stayed at home behind me and was fast asleep in bed.

Robert Louis Stevenson (1850–1894)

Now read these questions. You have a choice of four answers
to each question. Choose the *one* answer you think the best.
Draw a line in the box next to its letter, like this.

A ▭

61 Which sentence best sums up the poet's thoughts in line 2?

   A He is wondering why he can't see his shadow.
   B He is wondering why he can't see more of his shadow.
   C He is wondering what the point of his shadow is.
   D He is wondering how he can use his shadow.

A ▭
B ▭
C ▭
D ▭

61 ☐ 2

62 Lines 1 and 2 within each verse end with the same sound. In verse 1, for example,
these lines end with 'me' and 'see'. Which word below is used to describe words
that end with the same sound?

   A rhythm
   B rime
   C rhyme
   D rhymth

A ▭
B ▭
C ▭
D ▭

62 ☐ 2

MARK ☐

Comprehension

MARK

63 Which word best completes this sentence?

The second verse is about how the shadow grows and _____.

A shrinks ⟶ A ☐

B shoots ⟶ B ☐

C laughs ⟶ C ☐

D jumps ⟶ D ☐   **63**   2

64 Which word could be used instead of the phrase 'shoots' (line 7)?

A soars ⟶ A ☐

B bangs ⟶ B ☐

C climbs ⟶ C ☐

D slides ⟶ D ☐   **64**   2

65 Line 7 tells us that 'he sometimes shoots up taller like an india-rubber ball'. This is an example of which of the following?

A smile ⟶ A ☐

B personification ⟶ B ☐

C onomatopoeia ⟶ C ☐

D simile ⟶ D ☐   **65**   2

66 Which word could be used instead of the word 'notion' (line 9)?

A idea ⟶ A ☐

B movement ⟶ B ☐

C mystery ⟶ C ☐

D game ⟶ D ☐   **66**   2

67 Which is the correct spelling for how the child feels in line 12?

A embarist ⟶ A ☐

B embarased ⟶ B ☐

C embarrassed ⟶ C ☐

D embarassed ⟶ D ☐   **67**   2

68 The shadow stays close to the child (lines 11–12). Why do you think the shadow does this?

A The shadow is cowardly. ⟶ A ☐

B A shadow cannot leave. ⟶ B ☐

C The child dislikes the shadow. ⟶ C ☐

D The shadow is teasing the child. ⟶ D ☐   **68**   2

69 The last two lines of the poem describe how the shadow stayed in bed when the boy got up one day. Which phrase from the poem explains *why* the shadow stayed in bed?

A 'before the sun was up' (line 13) ⟶ A ☐

B 'like an arrant sleepy-head' (line 15) ⟶ B ☐

C 'stayed at home behind me' (line 16) ⟶ C ☐

D 'was fast asleep' (line 16) ⟶ D ☐   **69**   2

MARK

Comprehension

MARK

70 Which phrase best describes the child's attitude to the shadow?

- A annoyed and confused
- B amazed and perplexed
- C tired and ashamed
- D amused and impatient

A ☐
B ☐
C ☐
D ☐

70 ☐ 2

71 Which word in the poem means *someone who is easily scared*?

- A coward
- B arrant
- C shame
- D fool

A ☐
B ☐
C ☐
D ☐

71 ☐ 2

72 Which of the words below would best complete the sentence?

Robert Louis Stevenson has written a very _____ poem about
a shadow·

- A imaginary
- B imaginative
- C imagination
- D imagery

A ☐
B ☐
C ☐
D ☐

72 ☐ 2

73 When writing about the shadow, Stevenson gives it human characteristics.
What name is given to this method of writing?

- A impersonation
- B personality
- C personification
- D personalisation

A ☐
B ☐
C ☐
D ☐

73 ☐ 2

74 The time of day is important in this poem. Which of these words does *not* refer
to a time of day?

- A dawn
- B twilight
- C dusk
- D autumn

A ☐
B ☐
C ☐
D ☐

74 ☐ 2

75 The poem is written in four groups of lines, each composed of four lines. One word that
describes each group of four lines is *verse*. Which of the following is another word
for *verse*?

- A paragraph
- B stanza
- C section
- D chapter

A ☐
B ☐
C ☐
D ☐

75 ☐ 2

MARK ☐

COMPREHENSION SUB-TOTAL ☐ 30

Q. 76–85 Short writing task

MARK

Write for 20–30 minutes on *one* of the following. Continue on a separate sheet if you need to.

a) The last verse of the poem describes the very early morning. Imagine a day when you get up before sunrise. Describe your experience.

b) On an outing to the shops, you are sure that you are being followed by someone. What happens next?

c) Some people feel that today's children are over-protected and need to become more independent.
Write an article for a website aimed at nine to 12 year olds in which you argue *either* for *or* against this idea.

_____

_____

_____

_____

_____

_____

_____

_____

_____

_____

_____

_____

_____

_____

_____

_____

_____

_____

_____

_____

_____

_____

_____

END OF TEST

SHORT WRITING TASK SUB-TOTAL	10
English skills sub-total (from page 31)	60
Comprehension sub-total (from page 34)	30
Short writing task sub-total (from this page)	10
PAPER 10 TOTAL MARK	100

START HERE

Q. 1–60 English skills

MARK

Q. 1–5	Rewrite the text correctly, adding the necessary punctuation.	
punctuation	im not sure ill be able to come to mondays party kamran sighed the boy im afraid ive got a dental appointment at mr meltons surgery in oakwood	

1–5 ☐ 5

Q. 6–10	Add to the sentence a verb that is in the same word family as the word shown in capitals.	
verbs		

6 TOUGH   We _____ the box with more cardboard.   6 ☐ 1

7 DONOR   I _____ my pocket money to the charity.   7 ☐ 1

8 RIPE   When the grapes _____ we will pick them.   8 ☐ 1

9 MISTAKE   I am afraid you _____ my meaning.   9 ☐ 1

10 PACIFIC   I tried to _____ my angry neighbour.   10 ☐ 1

Q. 11–15	Write the *one* word that has *both* meanings.	
homonyms		

11 a primary colour / sad or miserable _____   11 ☐ 1

12 a violin / to swindle or cheat _____   12 ☐ 1

13 a series of steps / the act of running away or flying _____   13 ☐ 1

14 tree covering / noise a dog makes _____   14 ☐ 1

15 to keep finding fault with / a slang term for a horse _____   15 ☐ 1

MARK ☐

English skills   MARK

Q. 16–20	Add the *one* missing word.		
word meanings	16 A young tree is called a _____.	16	1
	17 A tin or box in which tea is kept is called a _____.	17	1
	18 People watching a sport are the _____.	18	1
	19 A person who rides horses professionally in races is a _____.	19	1
	20 A period of ten years is a _____.	20	1

Q. 21–25	Change the text from direct to indirect speech. For example, *"Can I book tickets online?" asked Dad* becomes *Dad asked if he could book tickets online*.		
direct to indirect speech	21 "What time is the last bus?" asked Josh.		
	_____	21	1
	22 "Can you tell me the way to the Town Hall?" the stranger asked me.		
	_____	22	1
	23 "Are those your gloves?" asked Nandita.		
	_____	23	1
	24 "Can you reach those biscuits for me?" asked the lady in the wheelchair.		
	_____	24	1
	25 "Will you marry me, Cinderella?" asked Prince Charming.		
	_____	25	1

Q. 26–30	Write the full county name that the abbreviation stands for.		
abbreviations	26 Herts _____	26	1
	27 S. Yorks _____	27	1
	28 Glos _____	28	1
	29 Cambs _____	29	1
	30 Leics _____	30	1

MARK

English skills

MARK

Q. 31–35	Write the popular phrase next to its meaning.	
popular phrases	lead the life of Riley, done to a turn, not to be sneezed at, rooted to the spot, a square peg in a round hole	
	31 unable to move _____	**31** ☐ 1
	32 someone not suited to a particular situation _____	
	_____	**32** ☐ 1
	33 live in great comfort _____	**33** ☐ 1
	34 shouldn't be turned down _____	**34** ☐ 1
	35 perfectly cooked _____	**35** ☐ 1

Q. 36–40	Read the clue. Fill in the missing letters to make the word.	
spelling	**36** an advantage or a favour	p _ _ _ _ _ _ _ e	**36** ☐ 1
	37 a boat with sails	y _ _ _ _	**37** ☐ 1
	38 the state of being married	m _ _ _ _ _ _ e	**38** ☐ 1
	39 yes, indeed	d _ _ _ _ _ _ _ _ y	**39** ☐ 1
	40 the second month	F _ _ _ _ _ _ y	**40** ☐ 1

Q. 41–45	Underline the adverb(s).	
adverbs	**41** She came early and spoke first.	**41** ☐ 1
	42 "I'm late!" shouted Mum, running fast down the path.	**42** ☐ 1
	43 He walks well but is in some pain.	**43** ☐ 1
	44 He is a very old man and walks slowly.	**44** ☐ 1
	45 There is the spot where the horse fell heavily.	**45** ☐ 1

MARK ☐

English skills

MARK

Q. 46–50	Complete the proverb or saying.		
proverbs and sayings	46 One man's meat _____ .	46	1
	47 All that glitters (or glisters) _____ .	47	1
	48 It's six of one _____ .	48	1
	49 Time and tide _____ .	49	1
	50 It never rains _____ .	50	1

Q. 51–55	Write out the sentence, correcting any errors.		
grammar	51 A second series of plays are being planned.		
	_____	51	1
	52 The escaped herd of cows are on the motorway.		
	_____	52	1
	53 A bunch of flowers are just what Mia needs.		
	_____	53	1
	54 The team were driving through town on an open-top bus.		
	_____	54	1
	55 The crew are in a state of shock.		
	_____	55	1

Q. 56–60	Read the clue. Fill in the missing letters to make the word.			
spelling	56 a group to decide things	c _ _ m _ _ _ _ e	56	1
	57 caring and hard-working	d _ d _ _ _ _ _ d	57	1
	58 the start	b _ _ _ _ _ _ _ _	58	1
	59 a low, indistinct sound	m _ _ _ _ _	59	1
	60 not relying on others	i n _ _ _ _ _ _ _ _ _	60	1

MARK

ENGLISH SKILLS SUB-TOTAL   60

Q. 61–75 Comprehension

MARK

Read this passage carefully.

A Garden for All

In this article, the latest in our series on garden design, Fiona Jones writes about the creation of outdoor spaces that will give special pleasure to those of us with limited sight.

Many people are surprised by how important gardens are to those whose vision is impaired. It is true that people who are blind or partially sighted cannot detect the visual features of a colourful
5 garden, such as the bright array of a rhododendron bush in full bloom or the ribbons of yellow and mauve formed by a field of springtime daffodils and crocuses. However, a garden can still provide great enjoyment for people who have lost their sight.
10 It takes knowledge and art to create any garden but additional skills are needed by gardeners who plant for those with sight loss.

The first thing is to create a safe garden – one in which the paths go in straight lines and over which
15 there are no hanging branches or planters at eye level to crash into. Paths should be wide enough to allow for guide dogs or users of white canes to move safely. Sharp edges and steps should be avoided, as should sunken ponds into which an unsuspecting
20 person could tumble.

Those who create gardens for the blind look most creatively at things to include as well as things to avoid. Landmarks – perhaps a sundial, a rippling water feature or wind chimes – are useful. All these
25 give definition to a space and help to remind people of where they are. People with impaired sight are often extra sensitive to sounds and scents and can enjoy the hum of bees and the sound of running water. Scented plants attract bees. Benches
30 placed near bee-friendly plants or water features can give great pleasure. Plants with different textures and which can be safely touched are fun. Many people with limited sight can make out pale-coloured flowers against dark backgrounds and
35 gardeners focusing on their needs are very inventive with light and shade. Fruit trees and bushes are easy to grow and everyone – whether sighted or not – enjoys eating an apple or a plum straight from the tree.

Now read these questions. You have a choice of four answers to each question. Choose the *one* answer you think the best. Draw a line in the box next to its letter, like this.

A ▭

61 Which phrase best completes the sentence?

Some people find it _____ that many blind people can enjoy gardens.

A extraordinary

B important

C invisible

D surprising

61 ▢ 2

62 Which of the following is *not* a flowering plant?

A rhododendron

B ribbon

C daffodil

D crocus

62 ▢ 2

MARK ▭

Comprehension

MARK

63 The words 'vision' and 'visual' (paragraph 1) have something to do with seeing.
    Which of the following words does *not* have anything to do with seeing?

    A invisible
    B virus
    C visibility
    D television

    63   2

64 Which phrase best completes the sentence?

    Those who design gardens for people with impaired sight need special _____.

    A art
    B knowledge
    C abilities
    D experience

    64   2

65 It is important to keep all of the following to a minimum in a garden for the blind.
    Which *one* word sums up all the others?

    A hazards
    B steps
    C dogs
    D ponds

    65   2

66 Which word could be used in place of the word 'unsuspecting' (line 19)?

    A unwary
    B expectant
    C trustworthy
    D careless

    66   2

67 Why are sundials, water features and wind chimes (lines 23–24) so helpful in a garden
    for the blind?

    A They give pleasure.
    B They sound attractive.
    C They make the garden more interesting.
    D They help people to work out where they are.

    67   2

68 Which of the words below would best complete the sentence?

    Even if visually impaired people cannot see much in gardens, they can derive much
    pleasure from using their other _____.

    A abilities
    B senses
    C sounds
    D sensitivities

    68   2

MARK

Comprehension

MARK

69 Identify the types of words contained in this sentence from lines 29–31.

'Benches placed near bee-friendly plants or water features can give great pleasure.'

A four nouns, three verbs and one adjective   A ☐
B three nouns, two verbs and three adjectives   B ☐
C five nouns, two verbs and two adjectives   C ☐
D four nouns, two verbs and one adjective   D ☐

69 ☐ 2

70 Which word has a similar meaning to 'inventive' as used in line 35?

A ingenuous   A ☐
B scientific   B ☐
C artistic   C ☐
D creative   D ☐

70 ☐ 2

71 Which of the phrases below would best complete the sentence?

The article focuses particularly on the fact that _____ enjoy a garden.

A blind and visually impaired people   A ☐
B there is more than one way to   B ☐
C blind people can't really   C ☐
D one has to work hard to help some people   D ☐

71 ☐ 2

Find the spelling mistake. Underline it and write the box letter at the end of the line.

72 Garden design is   not a straightforward   bisiness and requires   exceptional skill.

   A   B   C   D   ☐

72 ☐ 2

73 Designers and architects   must biuld for   the convenience   of everyone.

   A   B   C   D   ☐

73 ☐ 2

74 A plant expert   is a horticulturalist   and a tree spesialist   is an arboriculturalist.

   A   B   C   D   ☐

74 ☐ 2

75 Everyone has their   own view of what   makes a truely   memorable garden.

   A   B   C   D   ☐

75 ☐ 2

MARK ☐

COMPREHENSION SUB-TOTAL ☐ 30

Q. 76–85 Short writing task

MARK

Write for 20–30 minutes on *one* of the following. Continue on a separate sheet if you need to.

a) Imagine you have a blind or partially sighted visitor and you are showing them round your garden, local park or other outdoors area. Write the conversation you have with the visitor in which you describe what is around you.

b) You have moved into a new house with a large garden. You can design it and plant it in any way you like. Explain your plans.

c) Your local council has acquired a large piece of land and is inviting residents to suggest how it should be used. Write a letter in which you argue for *either* a new park *or* a new swimming pool *or* a new cinema complex.

43

_____

_____

_____

_____

_____

_____

_____

_____

_____

_____

_____

_____

_____

_____

_____

_____

_____

_____

_____

_____

_____

END OF TEST

SHORT WRITING TASK SUB-TOTAL	10
English skills sub-total (from page 39)	60
Comprehension sub-total (from page 42)	30
Short writing task sub-total (from this page)	10
PAPER 11 TOTAL MARK	100

Paper 12

Q. 1–60 English skills

MARK

Q. 1–5 punctuation	Rewrite the text correctly, adding the necessary punctuation. the play said paola is the importance of being earnest by oscar wilde have you seen it its very funny

1–5 ☐ 5

Q. 6–10 word meanings	Some colours are named after precious stones. Write down the colour of each item below. For example, *Amber is yellow.*

6 Ruby is _____ .

6 ☐ 1

7 Sapphire is _____ .

7 ☐ 1

8 Jet is _____ .

8 ☐ 1

9 Amethyst is _____ .

9 ☐ 1

10 Emerald is _____ .

10 ☐ 1

Q. 11–15 odd one out (by meaning)	Underline the *one* word that is the odd one out.

11 right, acute, obtuse, left

11 ☐ 1

12 stadium, theatre, arena, drama

12 ☐ 1

13 heart, liver, skin, tooth

13 ☐ 1

14 skate, scooter, ski, rollerblade

14 ☐ 1

15 beech, porch, maple, birch, larch

15 ☐ 1

MARK ☐

English skills

MARK

Q. 16–20 popular phrases	Write the popular phrase next to its meaning.		

out of the woods, to drown one's sorrows, to give up the ghost, to pull through, to push one's luck

16 to die _____   **16**   1

17 to try to get away with something _____   **17**   1

18 to survive _____   **18**   1

19 to drink a lot of alcohol in order to forget _____   **19**   1

20 free from difficulty _____   **20**   1

Q. 21–25 word meanings, spelling	Read the clue. Fill in the missing letters to make the word.		

21 the practice of spying   e _ _ _ _ _ _ _ _   **21**   1

22 not allowed by law   i _ _ _ _ _ _ _   **22**   1

23 the sending of thoughts from one mind to another t _ _ _ _ _ _ _ _ _   **23**   1

24 protecting the natural environment   c _ n _ _ _ _ _ _ t _ _ _   **24**   1

25 melted rock from under the earth   l _ _ _ _ or m _ _ _ _ _   **25**   1

Q. 26–30 adjectives	An adjective can be made from the noun shown in capitals. Write it in the phrase that is given.		

26 NORTHUMBERLAND   the _____ pipes   **26**   1

27 CUMBRIA   the _____ lakes and fells   **27**   1

28 BELGIUM   the _____ capital, Brussels   **28**   1

29 SPAIN   the _____ beaches   **29**   1

30 WALES   the _____ mountains   **30**   1

MARK

English skills

MARK

Q. 31–35

indirect to direct speech

Change the sentence from indirect to direct speech.
For example, *Levi said that he would text me when he arrives* becomes
"I'll text you when I arrive," said Levi.

31 Joanna shouted for the ball to be passed to her.

_____

| 31 | 1 |

32 Navid asked Dad when dinner would be ready.

_____

| 32 | 1 |

33 The actor hoped to work on stage, rather than in films.

_____

_____

| 33 | 1 |

34 Ailsa's mum invited me to join them on holiday.

_____

| 34 | 1 |

35 Karl admitted that he'd left his boots in the car.

_____

| 35 | 1 |

Q. 36–40

spelling

Read the clue. Fill in the missing letters to make the word.

36 discontented, not pleased   d _ _ _ _ _ _ _ _ _ _ d | 36 | 1 |

37 clumsy or ungraceful   a _ _ _ _ _ d | 37 | 1 |

38 a lengthy trip   j _ _ _ _ _ y | 38 | 1 |

39 to vanish from sight   d _ _ _ _ _ _ _ r | 39 | 1 |

40 likely to alter   c h _ _ _ _ _ _ _ _ | 40 | 1 |

Q. 41–45

adverbs

Add to the sentence an adverb that is made from the word shown in capitals.

41 BIGAMY   Zak was in jail after _____ marrying two women. | 41 | 1 |

42 HUNGER   At break-time she _____ ate the sandwich. | 42 | 1 |

43 BRUTE   The dog was treated _____ by its owner. | 43 | 1 |

44 ENIGMA   He smiled _____ but said nothing. | 44 | 1 |

45 EERIE   Lily's voice echoed _____ in the empty house. | 45 | 1 |

MARK [   ]

English skills

MARK

Q. 46–50 antonyms	Write down the antonym of the word.		
	46 summery _____	46	1
	47 wrongful _____	47	1
	48 sickness _____	48	1
	49 knowledge _____	49	1
	50 poverty _____	50	1

Q. 51–55 word choice	Put the occupation in the sentence where it makes the best sense. surgeon, bursar, IT manager, undertaker, steward		
	51 The _____ who organised the funeral was surprisingly jolly.	51	1
	52 The _____ who operated on my father did a brilliant job.	52	1
	53 My sister who loves computers is now an _____.	53	1
	54 The _____ on the plane was helpful when I lost my passport.	54	1
	55 My parents got the bill from the _____.	55	1

Q. 56–60 prefixes, spelling	The prefix *tri* means *three*. Fill in the missing letters to make the word.		
	56 A figure with three angles and three sides is a tri _ _ _ _ _.	56	1
	57 A sporting contest with three events is a tri _ _ _ _ _ _.	57	1
	58 The French flag of three colours is known as the tri _ _ _ _ _ _.	58	1
	59 A pedal-powered vehicle with three wheels is a tri _ _ _ _ _.	59	1
	60 The Roman God Neptune's three-pronged spear is a tri _ _ _ _.	60	1

MARK

ENGLISH SKILLS SUB-TOTAL   60

Q. 61–75 Comprehension

MARK

Read this passage carefully.

UP AND AWAY WITH BRACKEN'S BALLOONS

Bracken's Balloons has been operating Hot Air Balloon flights since 1957. We have a safety record that is second to none. Come and experience your first ever flight with us – it makes a uniquely special present – or you can enrol
5 on our pilot training course. We provide everything you need, including equipment, training, instruction and exams. Many people take their first flight and then sign up for a full course as soon as they touch down!

Weather
10 Safe ballooning depends on weather conditions. Stable weather (i.e. not thundery or cloudy) is essential and there should be no likelihood of rain. Determining the wind speed, which is measured in knots, is critical. On the ground, the wind speed should be 9 knots (around 11 miles per hour)
15 or under. At 600 metres above sea level it should be no more than 18 knots (around 21 miles per hour). Visibility must be good – ideally you should be able to see at least 5 kilometres all round you when you are airborne. All sensible balloonists check the forecast before they set off and keep a careful eye
20 on changes in the weather.

Your flight with Bracken's Balloons
Your pilot will be a trained and experienced professional balloonist. He will have undertaken a rigorous training course that involves:
25 i) a minimum of 16 hours' supervised flying
ii) a minimum of four flights with an approved instructor
iii) passing exams in five regulation subjects
iv) training in how to maintain good relationships with landowners.

30 ### How much is a single flight?
We have a range of options for those considering a flight. The fee for a single person flying on a weekday for one hour is as little as £120. An unforgettable flight for a party of 16 in one of our largest balloons, and lasting three hours (complete
35 with champagne and nibbles), will set you back no more than £1850. Consult our website, www.brackensballoons.org, to see the huge range of different ways in which you can have a sky-high experience with Bracken's Balloons.

Now read these questions. You have a choice of four answers to each question. Choose the *one* answer you think the best. Draw a line in the box next to its letter, like this.

A ▭

61 In 2007, Bracken's Balloons celebrated which anniversary?

A silver
B diamond
C ruby
D golden

61 ⬚ 2

62 What claim does Bracken's Balloons make about its safety record (lines 2–3)?

A It is very good.
B It is better than everyone else's.
C It is better than almost everyone's.
D It is exceptional.

62 ⬚ 2

MARK ▭

Comprehension

MARK

63 What is a 'uniquely special present' (line 4)?

    A the only present of its kind   A ☐

    B a wonderfully different gift   B ☐

    C a real treat for someone   C ☐

    D a very exciting gift   D ☐   63 2

64 Which of the following words does *not* have a similar meaning to 'pilot' (lines 5 and 22)?

    A captain   A ☐

    B helmsman   B ☐

    C steward   C ☐

    D steersman   D ☐   64 2

65 What is the meaning of 'touch down' (line 8)?

    A get airborne   A ☐

    B get inside   B ☐

    C feel safe   C ☐

    D land   D ☐   65 2

66 'Determining the wind speed, which is measured in knots, is critical' (lines 12–13). Which other word in this paragraph means the same as 'critical'?

    A stable (line 10)   A ☐

    B essential (line 11)   B ☐

    C good (line 17)   C ☐

    D sensible (line 18)   D ☐   66 2

67 For balloonists, which of the following is *not* an important weather consideration?

    A rain   A ☐

    B cloud   B ☐

    C sunshine   C ☐

    D wind   D ☐   67 2

68 What is the meaning of the word 'rigorous' as it is used in line 23?

    A energetic   A ☐

    B thorough   B ☐

    C difficult   C ☐

    D lengthy   D ☐   68 2

MARK

Comprehension

MARK

69 Which of the four elements of the training course do you think would involve learning about being considerate and tactful?

A i

B ii

C iii

D iv

A ☐
B ☐
C ☐
D ☐

69 ☐ 2

70 What is the purpose of the paragraph headed 'Your flight with Bracken's Balloons'?

A to inform the customers

B to reassure the customers

C to entertain the customers

D to persuade the customers

A ☐
B ☐
C ☐
D ☐

70 ☐ 2

71 Bracken's Balloons offers 'a range of options' (line 31). Which other word could be used here instead of 'options'?

A opportunities

B prices

C flights

D choices

A ☐
B ☐
C ☐
D ☐

71 ☐ 2

Find the spelling mistake. Underline it and write the box letter at the end of the line.

72 People appreciate the opportunaty of a silent flight over glorious countryside.

A B C D ☐

72 ☐ 2

73 Others feel anxious at being airborn without an engine or a parachute.

A B C D ☐

73 ☐ 2

74 Pigeons exhibit considerable suprise at a boxful of people floating past.

A B C D ☐

74 ☐ 2

75 The priciest option is costly but a definate possibility for a celebration.

A B C D ☐

75 ☐ 2

MARK ☐

COMPREHENSION SUB-TOTAL ☐ 30

Q. 76–85 Short writing task
MARK

Write for 20–30 minutes on *one* of the following. Continue on a separate sheet if you need to.

a) You are up in a balloon, flying over Sprocket Woods, Sprocket Lake and Stonecaster village and castle. Write the mobile phone texts that you are sending to your best friend to describe what you are seeing and feeling. You may abbreviate but your spelling must be correct.

b) You are a pigeon, unimpressed by the human beings occupying your space. Write the conversation you have with your fledglings when you return to your nest.

c) Ballooning is a safe activity when done responsibly. But many people enjoy far more risky activities. Are you attracted by adventurous sports such as sky diving, parachuting or rock climbing? Discuss your thoughts.

END OF TEST

SHORT WRITING TASK SUB-TOTAL   10

English skills sub-total (from page 47)   60

Comprehension sub-total (from page 50)   30

Short writing task sub-total (from this page)   10

PAPER 12 TOTAL MARK   100

Progress chart

Write the score (out of 100) for each paper in the box provided at the bottom of the chart. Then colour in the column above the box to the appropriate height to represent this score.

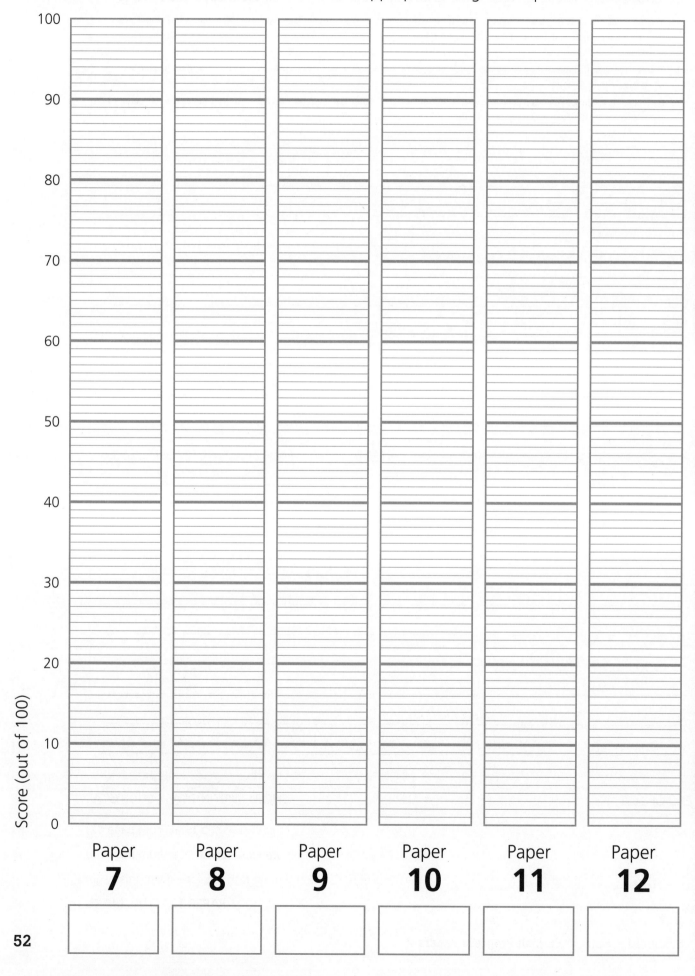

Score (out of 100)

| Paper 7 | Paper 8 | Paper 9 | Paper 10 | Paper 11 | Paper 12 |